Aberdeen
in old picture postcards volume 2

John Clark

European Library ZALTBOMMEL/THE NETHERLANDS

GB ISBN 90 288 6646 9

© 2001 European Library – Zaltbommel/The Netherlands

European Library
post office box 49
NL – 5300 AA Zaltbommel/The Netherlands
telephone: 0031 418 513144
fax: 0031 418 515515
e-mail:publisher@eurobib.nl

Introduction

Aberdeen on the Scottish coast has given its name to several towns in the USA but they are all modest in size compared with the original city. Aberdeen has been a settled area for two millennia and has now grown to about a quarter of a million residents. It is located between the sea and the mountains and has tended to look towards the sea for business opportunities, rather than developing land links. There was a bustling international trade from Aberdeen for centuries before there was a decent road to the city. The variety of livelihoods followed in the area, from quarrying through agriculture to textiles, has enabled Aberdeen to avoid some of the economic swings experienced elsewhere.

In 1989 I prepared a volume on the old postcards of Aberdeen, which reflected some of the changes that the city had seen in the previous ninety years. After a decade, during which the original volume was reprinted three times, we see more changes, particularly to shops, churches and cinemas. In preparing this volume of postcards of the city I have tried to avoid repeating views from our first volume, not always an easy task as the majority of cards show Union Street, the university, the harbour and the bridges. Since that publication, it has been evident that parts of the city are suffering from the attentions of the multinational and chain store. This is most regrettable as Union Street represents one of the greatest achievements in urban living in the islands. However, there are still many parts of the city that have scarcely changed in fifty years, the granite defying all attempts to spoil its appearance.

The English travel writer H.V. Morton had strong views on Aberdeen, which are worth repeating. 'A city built of the hardest known stone, in a part of the world which must be unfit for human habitation for several months of the year... this city seems to me like the world's greatest monument to that god who helps those who help themselves'. Aberdeen is a surprise to all people new to the city. It has had many nicknames over the years, including the Houston of Europe, but none of them prepare you for the scale and monumental nature of the place. The author Leila Abeulela, originally from Sudan, had heard that Aberdeen was the centre of the European oil industry. She says that she imagined 'skyscrapers and bustling streets but found Aberdeen'. This impact has been diminished in recent years by the developments along the main road to the south, but arriving by rail still retains that impact as one sweeps through miles of countryside and then pulls into a major city.

Aberdeen remains one of the most pleasant places to live in the country, with a bracing but healthy climate. It is large enough to have city amenities but still close to the sea and countryside. Its diverse economy, and the good fortune to be in the right place during the oil boom, has created a city that faces the future with confidence. This small volume celebrates the first half of the twentieth century in Aberdeen and provides an opportunity to note both change and continuity in the Granite City.

Acknowledgements
I wish to thank all the people who helped with the preparation of this small volume, particularly Mr. John Linklater and Mrs. Eileen Duncan, who lent cards from their collections. I have received valuable information from the House of Fraser, Marcliffe Hotel, the Convent of the Sacred Heart, the Royal Naval Reserve, Aberdeen Library Service, the National Railway Museum and several members of the family. I have found numerous books useful and have indicated where further information can be found on a couple of occasions. All the pictures are postcards over fifty years old as far as I am able to ascertain. If any errors appear they are the author's responsibility.

1 **Union Street**

The corner of Nicholas Street showing the Commercial Bank of 1936, a classical building by Jenkins and Marr. It is now the Royal Bank of Scotland. The Queen Victoria statue was still in place until 1964. The card was published in 1938.

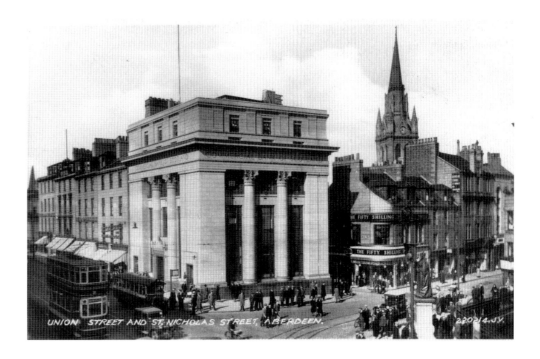

UNION STREET AND ST. NICHOLAS STREET, ABERDEEN.

2 *Castle Street*

Aberdeen Castle gave its name to this spot when this was the gate or gait to the fortifications. There are several interesting buildings grouped around this transport hub. We can see trams No. 6 (withdrawn 1926) and 79 and bus No. 8 (delivered 1921). The Thorncroft J bus was originally fitted with solid tyres and until 1925 retained paraffin lighting. A charabanc is nearly full of passengers.

Castle Street and Salvation Army Citadel, Aberdeen. 562

3 **Union Street**

'Hearty Greetings' says the banner to King Edward VII in 1906. We see the top of Union Street on the day that the University extension was opened.

4 Feast

On the evening that the new university building opened in 1906 the Chancellor of the University, Lord Strathcona, gave a banquet in Strathcona Hall, a temporary building put up on Gallowgate. The hall allowed 2500 to dine, cost £3400 and witnessed the greatest feast that the city has seen. Such was the snobbery of the day that the menu was entirely in French and only foreign alcohol was offered. Clearly a good deal of alcohol was consumed because that following day the Rector had some sharp words on the subject.

Photo by MacMahon, Aberdeen. · TABLES SET FOR BANQUET, STRATHCONA·HALL.   G. L. M'Keggie, Aberdeen.

5 St. Nicholas Street

There are many views of St. Nicholas Street but this one is unusual in that it shows a small hut on the bridge. A notice reads 'Recruiting and enquiry office. Gordon Highlanders, Royal Field Artillery, Royal Engineers, Royal Army Medical Corps'. We can safely date this card to the Great War.

St. Nicholas Street and Queen's Statue, Aberdeen

6 Old Grey Friars Church

The kirk was built in 1530 under the direction of Bishop Gavin Dunbar. It was a modest structure only 118 feet by 26 feet and used sandstone. It was originally occupied by an order of Franciscans. Unfortunately it stood in the way of the expansion of the University and was demolished in 1903. Some fragments were saved and the east window was built into the new Greyfriars, which stands alongside the university frontage.

Old Greyfriars Parish Church. ABERDEEN.

7 Union Street

A snow scene in Union Street shows dozens of men digging out the tramway. This is probably the great storm of December 1908, when over seven hundred men were employed to clear snow from the city.

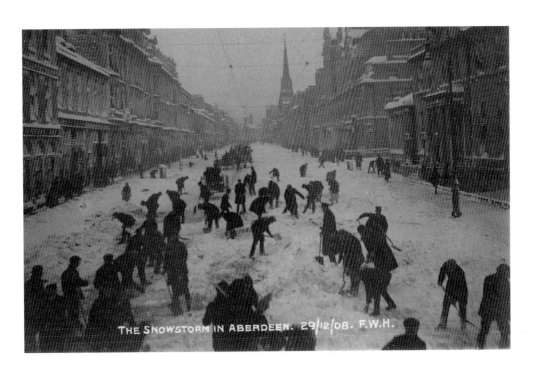

THE SNOWSTORM IN ABERDEEN. 29/12/08. F.W.H.

8 Coronation

King George V had his Coronation on Friday 23 June 1911. A Pageant celebrating the Battle of Hawlaw of 1411 was organized in Aberdeen.

CORONATION PROCESSION, ABERDEEN, SCENES FROM HARLAW PAGEANT   THE ADELPHI SERIES.
C. H. & S. A.

9 **Coronation**

This card reads 'A reminder of 22.6.1911'. The rider was a member of the Coronation procession that day. Published by E.M. Middleton, 181 Union Street.

10 John Falconer & Co

Falconer's was founded by Alexander Falconer in Narrow Wynd in 1788, moving to Queen Street in 1801. It was inherited as John Falconer and Co on his death in 1828 by three nephews. They moved to 23 Union Street.

In 1871 his nephew George became sole proprietor, whose son William assumed that position in 1889. In 1871 the business leased the ground floor of the Royal Hotel, part of the existing building at 65 Union Street and purchased the entire whole Royal Building in 1883. Various enlargements added Ladies Outfit-ting and home furnishings and the staff grew to about 80. The company traded until 1952 selling everything, from kilts to afternoon teas, when the House of Fraser took over, keeping the name until 1975. The store has been extensively enlarged and modernized over the years, maintaining over two hundred years of service.

11 Crown Street Post Office

The Post office was designed by J. Cumming Wyness and opened by the Postmaster General Sydney Buxton in 1907. It shows the Balmoral influence common to several buildings of the period. As an economy measure Sunday deliveries stopped from January 1909.

V 263-8   ABERDEEN, NEW POST OFFICE   RAPID PHOTO. E C

A sandstone building dating from 1817, the kirk added a chancel in 1880 and it has been remodelled several times since. Critics have said that it is the best recent work in the city. It is an austere structure in Craigleith ashlar that is softened by various coats of arms in the aisles. It is recognized as the mother church of the American Episcopal Church as Bishop Seabury of the USA had been consecrated in 1784, in an earlier building. The Seabury memorial stone was laid in 1938 by the American Ambassador Joe Kennedy accompanied by his son, the future President John F. Kennedy.

THE NAVE, St. ANDREW'S CATHEDRAL, ABERDEEN

13 *Watt and Grant*

Watt and Grant, located at 221 Union Street from 1882, was the foremost fashion store in Aberdeen. It was open from 1882 until 1981 on the corner of Dee Street.

WATT & GRANT'S
LUNCHEON
AND
TEA ROOMS
ABERDEEN.

14 *Babbie Law's*

1885 the lady licensee Babbie Law left this spot which still bears her name. Granite workers would drop in to lay the dust whilst carting blocks from Rubislaw quarry to the city centre. A branch of Chivas the grocers can be seen on the left. This 1930's view show more up to date vehicles than that in volume one and one of the new Balesha beacons.

HOLBURN JUNCTION ("BABBIE LAW") ABERDEEN

6

15 *George Street*

Named after King George III, we can see Watt and Co ironmongers on the right and School Hill on the left. The first electric trams ran from here on 22 December 1898.

GEORGE STREET, ABERDEEN.

The prominent Palace Hotel, by Union Bridge, was damaged beyond repair by a fire during which six staff lost their lives. It started on 31 October 1941, in the Grill Room. Final demolition took place in 1950. The hotel, built in 1874 for Pratt & Keith, drapers, had been a North of Scotland Railway hotel from 1891 and was taken over by the LNER in 1923. A view of the exterior can be found in volume 1. Interiors are far less common.

DINING ROOM, PALACE HOTEL, ABERDEEN.

17 Pirie's

Posted in 1908 to London, Mr. Pirie wrote to order 'Varberg Nappe gloves at 21 shillings and nine pence'. His advertising postcard offers among other goods 'Veilings, Dainty Neck-wear and Golf Jerseys'. Mr. Pirie passed away on 7 July 1911 aged 47. His home had been at 68 Cairnfield Place. He was the son of Thomas Pirie, Newmills, Keith, and had learnt his trade in Glasgow, returning to Aberdeen about 1900. He took over the Tartan Warehouse in Union Street and attended closely to his business rather than public affairs. He left a widow and young son.

PIRIE'S Fancy Drapery Warehouse,
133 Union Street, ABERDEEN.

THE NOTED SPECIALIST FOR
Everything Fashionable & Nice in Gloves, Blouses, Belts, Veilings,
Dainty Neck-Wear, Lace Goods, Umbrellas, Underskirts,
Golf Jerseys, Hosiery, &c., &c.
Write or Call on PIRIE. . . .

The whole of the golden age of postcards, politics were rather different to today. In 1884 two Labour members were elected to the Town Council and their numbers had risen to eight by 1919. They did not become the majority party until 1945. At a parliamentary level the Liberals were well in control for most of the time covered by this collection. Not that all elections were well supported, only 12% of the electorate voted during the first election for the education authority in 1919.

ABERDEEN.
THE CASTLEGATE on an ELECTION DAY.

19 *West Church*

The original nave of St. Nicholas was a ruin before 1745 when troops under the Duke of Cumberland stabled their horses in it. The present building was completed in 1755 to a design by James Gibb. The card shows the barrel-vaulted roof and some of the fine oak furniture. This is the Town Kirk and the venue for civic events with canopied seat for the Lord Provost. The East Church and the tower are a hundred years younger.

Interior West Church, Aberdeen

Adelphi Series

20 *Tea Room*

Typical of many dining rooms in Aberdeen, this one was the Alexandra Café, 11A Market Street. The card was posted in 1907 to Sergeant Major W.O.W. Gordon by his niece Nell Hay, who writes that she is working there.

THE DINING-ROOM, ALEXANDRA CAFE, 11A MARKET STREET, ABERDEEN.

21 *Regent Quay*

The frontage was completed in 1834 with further changes at the turn of the century. Along the quay we can see the Customs House built about 1779 and originally a private house. What changes have been witnessed from this spot! The small craft working cargo is the Sentinel.

V 263-6   ABERDEEN   REGENT QUAY   RAPID PHOTO. E C

Beyond the coal sacks three Aberdeen Steam Navigation Company ships are in view, unfortunately no names can be seen.

The structure of the nearest ship makes me believe that she is S.S. Harlaw. She had been built as the Swift in 1911 and was in the Aberdeen company from 1929 to 1946, surviving until 1963 abroad. An 1100-ton vessel, she had earlier survived damage by aircraft off Aberdeen in 1940.

THE HARBOUR, ABERDEEN

23 *Harbour*

This is a busy scene at the harbour with timber as the main cargo.

ADN 36   THE HARBOUR, ABERDEEN   A TUCK CARD

24 *Fittie Ferry*

Harbour ferries, such as this one from Footie to Torry, survived in several ports, including Bristol, well into the 20th century. The Footie ferry was used until the 1930s. In the nineteenth century Footdee had a large number of public houses including the Ferry Boat Inn run by Willie Cormack. The local joke was that the pubs never opened because they never closed.

No. 96   THE FITTIE FERRY. ABERDEEN.   ADELPHI SERIES
C. H. & S. A.

25 S.S. *Intaba*

S.S. Intaba was launched in 1910 for the J.T. Rennie Co. They had been in business since 1849 and ran steamers on the Aberdeen Direct Line from 1882. Their ships were painted with French grey hulls and yellow funnels, using African tribal names. The launch was delayed for forty-five minutes when the vessel stuck on the slipway. A variety of means were employed to move her. Three steam tugs put lines to her, a hydraulic jack was put in place and large numbers of workmen ran up and down the deck in unison to create a tremor in the hull. When she moved a Miss Byron, a daughter of one of the partners, smashed a carafe of wine on the hull. Intaba was the first vessel constructed by the Isherwood system on the North East Coast. The ship was built in eight and half months and carried 70 First Class and 60 Second Class passengers to Durban, South Africa. The company was taken over by J. & T. Harrison of Liverpool in 1911 who sold Intaba in 1927. A Burmese company used her until 1943 when she was scrapped in Ghent.

Launch of the S.S. "Intaba," 6th Sept., 1910.

Largest Vessel built in Aberdeen—length 401 ft., 4700 tons.

26 S. S. G. Koch

This may appear to be the wreck of a sailing ship but she was actually a Danish steamer, which went aground at Girdleness on 12 January 1913. The ship had been running out of coal and the crew had started to burn the cargo of pit props when she came ashore. Coastguards from Torry and Cove managed to fire lifelines to her to secure a breeches buoy and saved some of the crew. Seven men lost their lives.

Wreck of the S.S. "G. Koch" off Girdleness, Aberdeen   "Adelphi Series"

27   *Sheerlegs, the harbour*

Designed to lift heavy loads, more than one set of sheerlegs has been used in Aberdeen harbour. This set was made in 1910 to assist with construction and fitting out of S.S. Intaba, which will be found elsewhere. The sailing craft and small steamer are typical of this period.

The Harbour, Aberdeen.

28 *Mitchel's*

A trade directory of 1905-1906 shows an Andrew Mitchel and Co as Wholesale Fish Merchants on the North esplanade. We assume that this is his family business and note the smart collars and ties and the Newfoundland dog.

29 *Earl of Aberdeen*

The Earl of Aberdeen was typical of the vessels owned by the Aberdeen, Newcastle and Hull Steam Co Ltd. She was built by Hall Russell in 1889 and was a 210 feet long electrically illuminated craft. The open bridge offered little protection to the helmsman. The card dates from about 1910 when the First Class fare to London, on this 36-hour voyage, was one pound ten shillings. The same company's Highlander maintained the service until the 1930's but the Aberdeen Steam Navigation Company Ltd offered a passenger service to London until 1948.

Fitty, Footdee, Fittie or
Footie has had a variety of
ways of spelling its name
but always retains its own
strong character. Early in
the nineteenth century a
planned village was built
around North and South
with Pilot Square added
later. These provided modest homes for the fishing
community with sheds in
the centre offering space
to repair nets and other
land-based tasks. Alter-
ations over the years have
created a unique 'regulated
disorder'.

72   Harbour Channel and Beach from Torry, Aberdeen   Adelphi Series

31 H.M.S. Clyde

A 14 gun training ship was a familiar sight in the harbour for many years. A display of cannons and cutlasses was a tourist attraction. A Fifth Rate frigate, the Clyde, was built about 1820 and served in Aberdeen from September 1870 until June 1904. A number of cards exist in two forms with Clyde removed to make the cards appear more modern.

H. M. S. "Clyde".   Aberdeen Harbour.

32 Columbia

This card was posted on 20 June 1905 and shows the steam trawler A300 'Columbia' ashore at Aberdeen. Columbia was a 183-ton vessel built by Hall, Russell & Co in 1901. She was 108 feet long with a triple expansion steam engine. She appears to have survived this grounding whilst in the service of the Eastern Steam Fishing Co Ltd.

Steam Trawler "Columbia" ashore off Aberdeen

33 Morning work

Most cards of fishwives show smiling faces, surprising when you consider what hard work was involved.

Aberdeen Market. "Morning Work."

J. R. R. E.

34 Loading potatoes

Published by C. Raeburn & Co (Kerrs) Seed and Potato Merchants of Banff when the population was so small that their telephone number was Banff 49. These are identified as early potatoes for London and The Argentine. The boxes are marked Arran Cairn. It must have been a red-letter day when potatoes were sent to South America from where the crop originated.

LOADING 1,200 BAGS EARLY POTATOES TO LONDON, AND 40 CASES TO THE ARGENTINE, FROM ABERDEEN DOCKS

35 S.S. Argosy

The Argosy, a small steamer, only 406 tons, was involved in an accident on 17 January 1912. She was on her way from London, when her Master, Captain Peterson, attempted to enter Aberdeen Harbour during a storm. Her steering gear failed just as she neared the harbour entrance and the crew were helpless as she came ashore on the beach. 500 people hauled the Aberdeen lifeboat to the beach. This was a pulling or rowing boat named Bon Accord and she was successfully launched and the Argosy's crew was taken to safety. Unlike the S.S. Koch, the Argosy was on sand and it was possible to salvage her in due course.

STORM AT ABERDEEN BEACH: WRECK OF S.S. "ARGOSY"

W. H. & CO., LD.

36 Buksburn

The card appears to date from immediately after the war, with a new Land Rover in view. The Clydesdale and North of Scotland Bank is now simply the Clydesdale Bank in the same building. The Aberdeen Savings Bank building has gone.

BUCKSBURN LOOKING SOUTH.

37 **Cow on the beach**

This postcard reads that the photograph was taken on 22nd June 1932 and continues 'One of the novelties of Aberdeen. This great bull is very tame and takes visitors for a ride on the seafront'.

38 *Ballroom*

The Ballroom was designed by Thomas Roberts and Hume and won architectural prizes. The dance hall, shops and other facilities were constructed from 1927 at a cost of over £50,000.

The Dance Hall and Promenade, Aberdeen.

39 *Spectators at beach*

The spectators may be watching the Piorotts to be seen in volume 1.

THE BEACH AND BATHING STATION, ABERDEEN.

40 *Victorian costume at beach*
The card says that these are
Piel Islanders on holiday in
Aberdeen. It shows a col-
lection of hats, bonnets,
caps and a bowler, all making sure that these holiday-
makers do not get too
much sun.

41 The Prom

Pony rides, swings, a roundabout and a boating pond all appear on this card, posted in 1915. People enjoyed themselves in a low technology way in those days.

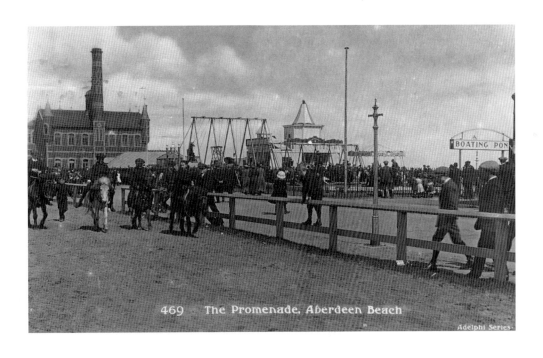

469   The Promenade, Aberdeen Beach

Adelphi Series

42 *Sandcastles*

On Childrens' Day, 5 July 1911 there was a heat wave reaching 81° F in the shade. 20,000 attended the sandcastle building competition near the bathing station. Such was the heat that a lot of fish at the market was only fit for manure.

CHILDREN'S DAY AT THE BEACH, ABERDEEN,   THE ADELPHI SERIES, C. H. & S. A.

43 *Funfair*

A 1930's card shows the funfair on the beach. Built by the American John Henry Iles, it burnt down on 5 December 1940.

PLEASURE PARK · BEACH · ABERDEEN

44 Picnic

'Picnic Aberdeen 1909' is written on the card. Unfortunately we cannot identify this charming family group.

45 *Bishop Grant*

Bishop Grant was briefly Roman Catholic Bishop of Aberdeen in 1889, based at St. Mary of the Assumption, Huntly Street. The building dates from 1860 when there were about 100 Catholics in a city of 74,000 residents. Alexander Ellis designed it when there were only two other Catholic churches in Aberdeen, including Woodside Church (to be seen in vol. 1). A spire by R.G. Wilson was added in 1876-1877 and the parish church became a cathedral in 1878. The cathedral was extensively modernized in 1960 and the altar is now a massive piece of Aberdeen granite. It is said that Catholicism in Aberdeen is unique in Scotland in that its presence was continuous and unbroken. Evidence for this includes a secret chapel in Provost Skene's House.

The late Right Rev. COLIN C. GRANT, D.D.,
Bishop of Aberdeen.
Cons. 1889. Died same year.

H.V. Morton claimed that in one of these granite buildings there was a secret Aberdeen Joke Office, which produced an endless stream of tales. He suggested that all the stories about Aberdonian attitude towards money were a careful propaganda ploy to keep the city's name before the world. In reality the Municipal and County Building dates from the 1870s and housed various local government offices.

V.71 ABERDEEN. MUNICIPAL BUILDINGS. RAPID PHOTO CO

47 *Gordon statue*

Charles George Gordon (1833-1885) was born down in Woolwich and earned a reputation for military competence in China in 1864. Gordon was a man of strong beliefs and worked in Egypt and the Sudan in opposing slavery in the 1870's. He gave his spare time in Britain to what we would now call social work. In 1884 he was given confusing instructions but was told to return to Sudan, where he would encounter the *Mahdi* Mohammed Ahmed. Gordon became trapped in Khartoum for nearly a year and when the rebel forces became aware of a relieving army, the rebels attacked the city and Gordon lost his life.

48   *Dr. Rannie*

Dr. Robert Rannie died on 15 August 1931 shortly after retiring. He was an Aberdeen University graduate and served as Medical Officer for Drumoak and surrounding districts before becoming School's Medical Officer for the Means. We suggest that it is time we revived this type of card to remember people who have served the public.

Dr. Robert Rannie.
Medical Practitioner, Peterculter, Aberdeenshire,
1888-1921.

49 *Marcliffe Hotel*

The Marcliffe Hotel was set up in 1951 on Queen's Terrace, boasting a unique tartan lounge. Margaret and Clifford Jordan established it. Mr. Jordan had been a dance bandleader in the Tivoli Theatre and it was initially used as a guesthouse by visiting theatrical folk. Between 1959 and 1979 Mr. A.P. Brown of Frazerburgh owned the hotel and he expanded the business both in size and facilities. He sold to Mr. J. Stewart Spence who developed it further. The old building has been replaced by office developments but the name is retained in the Marcliffe at Pitfodels.

Marcliffe Hotel, Aberdeen.

50 *Caledonian Hotel*

The Caledonian Hotel was built as the Grand Hotel and opened in 1892. White Kemnay granite was used for the construction in Italian renaissance style architecture. The hotel changed its name in 1930 when a syndicate of local businessmen purchased it for £50,000. This was a bargain as it cost £80,000 to build in the first place. The Caledonian is rightly proud of its ability to attract the finest clientele, including politicians, film stars and royalty. H.R.H. the Queen, Sir Anthony Eden and Clark Gable were all entertained at the Caledonian.

CALEDONIAN HOTEL, ABERDEEN

51 Forester Hill Hospital

Forester Hill was the brainchild of Professor Matthew Hay, who began planning the hospital complex in 1920. He was a distinguished figure who served as Aberdeen's Medical Officer for many years. The new Royal Infirmary, which included this smart kitchen, finally opened on 24 September 1936. School children were given a day's holiday but probably did not appreciate the economies of scale achieved by several hospitals sharing facilities including radiography, laundry and nurse training services.

THE KITCHEN, NEW ROYAL INFIRMARY, FORRESTERHILL, ABERDEEN

PRESS & JOURNAL PHOTO

52   Forester Hill Hospital

In 1927 the Lord Provost began the fund raising needed for the new hospital. In those pre-NHS days every community had to fend for itself. Among money raising ideas was the sale of postcards by the Press and Journal, of which this and the previous card are two examples. In all £525,000 was raised by public donations to meet the full cost of the 500-bed hospital.

A STORE ROOM IN THE NEW ROYAL INFIRMARY, FORRESTERHILL, ABERDEEN

53 *Gas loco*

Aberdeen Corporation Gas works between 1914 and 1918 used this steam locomotive. They needed an additional engine to cover the extra demands, which occurred during the war. The city paid £1164 and was canny enough to sell her at £1800. The shunter's cylinders were 14 inch in diameter and you can see from the maker's nameplate that Andrew Barclay Sons of Kilmarnock built her.

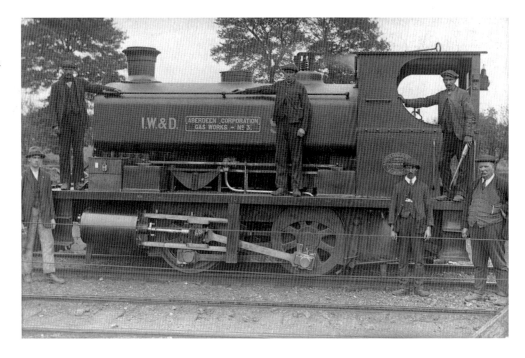

54 *Fish train*

The Up Train is leaving Aberdeen hauled by Nᵒ. 9899 Jeannie Deans and Nᵒ. 6394 Lord James of Douglas, which were both 4-4-0's. The marketing of fish took off with the arrival of the railway line. Lorries until did not challenge railway deliver after 1930.

55 LNER 6889

This engine is seen at Kittybrewster in August 1933. The locomotive was one of a class of nine, Class G10, built in 1893 by Neilsen and Co. An 0-4-4 design, the driving wheels were five feet in diameter, and she weighed 53 tons when full including two tons of coal. She was rebuilt with a new boiler in 1921. These engines were all based at Kittybrewster and worked the Aberdeen suburban services until April 1937 when the service was withdrawn. They ran to Dyce and Culter and occasionally as far a Banchory or Boddam. When the engine's 'subby' service days were over it had a brief spell at Thornton down in Fife as the Kirkcaldy pilot engine, before ending its working life as the pilot at Keith. It was scraped in 1940 after 47 years of service.

56 Joint Station

The foundation stone of the new Joint Railway Station building was laid on 28 May 1913 and by July the following year all the new platforms were in use. 190 men worked on the demolition of the old building and construction of this one. The bulk of the material is Freestone from Northumberland but some Kemnay granite is used. The concourse has a glass and steel roof measuring 245 by 97 feet. Either side of the train indicator board stairs provided access to the suburban lines. Behind the main bookstall, shown in this view, were the stationmaster and tele-graph offices. There were separate parcel offices for the Caledonian Railway and the North British Railway. A modern feature was an electric clock system synchronized from a mas-ter clock in the booking office. The card was posted in 1934.

INTERIOR, THE JOINT STATION, ABERDEEN.   86597.J.V.

57 *Woodside Station*

The message on this card says that it was taken in the summer of 1912. The writer, who unfortunately does not identify himself, says that it is his wife on the platform. The Highland Railway sent two engines to Inverness every day, at this period. The GNS did likewise with two services. According to the card this engine is returning to Inverness with the 2.20 PM Express from Aberdeen. The station opened in 1858 using the drained bed of the Woodside Canal and closed on 5 May 1937.

58 *Salmon fishers*

This card was posted 1911 when Aberdeen Harbour Board Fishing Committee reported a small fall on the previous catch, 54,015 pounds of salmon worth £4,444.17s. 9 d. Two years later came the six-hundredth anniversary of the grant of fishing rights by Robert the Bruce.

SALMON FISHING ON THE DEE, ABERDEEN.   1102

59 *Odd Fellows Hall*

Bolton Unity Friendly Society established or absorbed local lodges early in the twentieth century, at which time there were about 59 lodges in the city. Local lodges objected to conditions imposed by Bolton Unity's HQ in Manchester, and in 1889 they established an independent society, the Caledonian Order of United Oddfellows. The Oddfellows remained important until the 1950's, with an Oddfellows hall in Belmont Street until 1943. More detail can be found in a good history 'Trade Unionism in Aberdeen 1878-1900', K.D. Buckley (Edinburgh 1955).

THE ANCIENT NOBLE ORDER OF UNITED ODD FELLOWS

1832

BOLTON UNITY
FRIENDLY SOCIETY

Bon-Accord Lodge, 657.

A SOCIAL EVENING, to inaugurate the new Meeting Place of the Lodge, will take place on THURSDAY, the 13th June, to commence at Eight o'clock.

Tickets—Threepence.   (No Juveniles.)

Will be pleased to have members and their wives with us on that occasion.

J. MACKIE, *Secy.*

Car 129 was delivered in October 1929 and according to a note on the card was photographed on 8 April 1939. It is described as a Bush all enclosed 40/26 with a Peckham P35 motor. The vehicle was fitted with airbrakes about this time. It had a steel frame with a teak superstructure and remained in service until early 1957. It was an act of corporate vandalism when all the city's remaining trams were deliberately burned in May 1958.

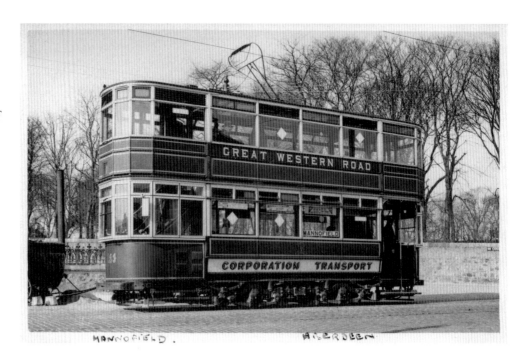

61 *Women on trams*

World War One created a shortage of male labour in a number of areas including the corporation tramways. When it became known that women would undertake traditional male jobs there was a meeting opposing such a move. In spite of such reaction women were recruited by Aberdeen Corporation from May 1915, initially as 'conductorettes'. By the end of the war nearly all the conductors and a handful of drivers were female. This card shows the pioneering group.

Aberdeen's First Eight Female Car Conductors.

This card was one sent by an autograph hunter, called Reginald Bray, part of a series sent to all the mayors in Britain. Obviously he did not get the title right. The card was signed and returned by the Lord Provost James Walker. Mr. Walker had been a successful businessman in the fish trade before he served as Lord Provost from 1902 to 1905. He was an active man involved in the Police Force and the construction of the Fish Market on Albert Quay. Walker Park is named after him.

63 Map

This card with a Cults
postmark of 1909 shows
part of a Bartholomew
map. It is representative of
a variety of cards showing
composite pictures, pull-
outs with a series of views,
hold-to-light cards and
other novelties. We can see
that both Bervie and Alford
had rail services at this
date.

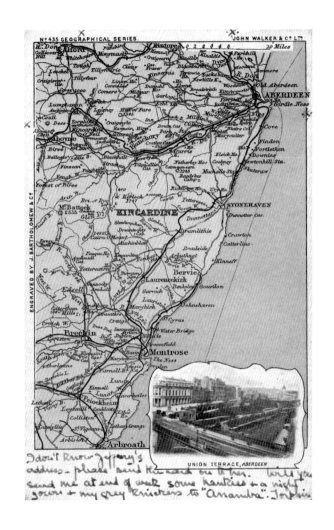

64 *Girdleness Lighthouse*

Girdleness Lighthouse was built by one of the Lighthouse Stephensons, Robert Stephenson, in 1833. 189 steps take you to the top of the 130-foot high tower. It still warns vessels up to nautical 19 miles away, but like all British lighthouses is no longer manned.

GIRDLENESS AND BAY OF NIGG, ABERDEEN FROM THE AIR

65 *Kingseat Mental Hospital*

Newmacher was built early in the century in the style of Alt Scherbitz or villa style. It occupied 337 acres of Kingseat estate, which had been purchased for £6,250. It opened on 16 May 1904 at a total cost of £125,000. It was this first hospital in the UK with this lay out having five blocks for each gender including six closed wards. Additional villas were built later and in 1930 responsibility was transferred from the Parish Council to Aberdeen City. By 1938 patient numbers had risen to 735. It as requisitioned during the Second World War.

Kingseat Asylum

66 New Poor House

A boys' reformatory opened on this site in 1857, with 50 lads under the control of a Governor and a Matron. It took its name from the Oldmill farm. In 1900 the land was sold to the parish council. In time the boys were moved out and a new structure erected with a viaduct to the main road. Naturally the women and men were accommodated in separate wings of the New Poor House which was opened on 15 May 1907. In keeping with the spirit of the age, life has been described as 'spartan but not intentionally un-kind'.

The New Poorhouse for Aberdeen

R. G. J.

67 *Oldmill Hospital*

The new Poor House became Oldmill Military Hospital from 1915 to 1919. A different view in Volume One shows a parade in the grounds. In this view a figure guards the gatehouse. After the war the general hospital concentrated on the sick poor and the special hospital became a TB unit. It was taken over by the city council and named Woodend (Municipal) Hospital in 1927. Many improvements followed. Since 1989 it has been a centre for non-urgent orthopaedic surgery and geriatric care. The other departments for oncology, general surgery and so forth moved to Forester Hill.

Entrance to Oldmill Military Hospital, Aberdeen.

68   *City Hospital*

Cards of the City Hospital are uncommon. It was built as the Cunningar Hospital in 1877, a fever hospital, the clock and bell being transferred from the water house. When Aberdeen was struck by an outbreak of typhoid fever in May and June of 1964, this hospital was the centre of the city's fight back against the infection. There were over 500 victims of the fever but only one death, a tribute to the quality of care offered by the medical and nursing staff.

City Hospital, Aberdeen.

69 Leadside Street

Leadside Street was laid out on part of the Gilcomston property. The name refers to the lade or stream which ran from Gilcomston dam to the Gilcomston Mills at the top of Jack's Brae. It was drained and filled about 1907. This is one of the oldest granite-built streets.

Leadside Road, Aberdeen   R. G. J.

70 Short Loanings

Loaning is a country road, it is a long time since this part of the city was in the country. Nearby, Craigie Loanings is an other road, which uses the same name. This view shows fore stairs, which were once very much a part of Scottish architecture but are now rarely seen. In 1861 the Census showed that 345 of all Scottish dwellings had only one room and 37% had two rooms. Many would have been of this appearance.

In Short Loanings, Aberdeen   R. G. J.

71 *Westburn Road*

Westburn Road on a quiet day with one figure wandering down the middle of the road.

WESTBURN ROAD, ABERDEEN.

2027

In our hectic age we find it surprising that a scene with such little activity was considering worth recording. It is clear that cards of smaller streets were produced in only modest quantities compared with Union Street and so forth.

Great Western Place, Aberdeen

73 Tivoli Tonics 1934

The Tivoli Theatre, originally Her Majesty's, in Guild Street, no longer provides an entertainment such as this. Dave Willis first came to fame in 1925 leading the fun at shows called the Tivoli Tonics, which remained the title of the Spring Show for many years. Willis was a 'Master of unrelated nonsense' radiating good humour. Others saw him as Scotland's Charlie Chaplin with the stamp of comic genius, who practised good clean comedy. He retired from theatrical life in 1951, apart from a brief come back in 1956.

Dave Willis' "Tivoli Tonics" 1934

74 *Mannofield Church*

Aberdeen had horse-drawn trams but these were replaced by electric trams from 1899, the Mannofield route changing in 1902. Originally open-topped, the trams were largely covered over by 1909. This obviously converted tram is seen in front of Mannofield Church, which at the time this was posted in 1918 there were few houses beyond it. The church replaced a wooden building and seats 700 but when it opened on 30 July 1883 there were only 92 communicants. The West window is dedicated to Miss Gordon, who died in 1892. The wooden church was used in other sites before being demolished in 1969.

Published by E. GROUNDWATER

Mannofield Parish Church, Aberdeen

75 *Beaconsfield Place*

Typical of the West End feud out by the City of Aberdeen Land Association. Critics have said that only the building materials distinguish such homes from property of similar date elsewhere in Britain.

76 *Dermaline Road*

Many cards were produced in small quantities, such as this one posted by Mrs. Skinner at No. 4 to Mrs. Tough, School Road Old Aberdeen in 1904.

77   Distillery fire

There have been several distilleries in Aberdeen including the North of Scotland Distillery that was destroyed by fire in 1904. Over 88,000 gallons of whisky, valued at one shilling and six pence per gallon, was lost and total damage was estimated at £108,000. The distillery in Hardgate belonged to Daluaine-Talisker Distilleries Ltd. and burned for over twelve hours. It is believed that a workman accidentally started the fire whilst trying to repair a barrel. Soon a blazing stream of spirit poured from the bonded warehouse down to the Ferry Hill Burn and the city sewage system. The scene was described as a perfect inferno with the spirituous flames almost free of smoke, belching forth with ever increasing fury. Leaping from the ground 'as from a huge Christmas pudding... the flames swirled and twisted with lightning like rapidity into the most extraordinary forms imaginable'.

Fire at the North of Scotland Distillery, Aberdeen, 27th Sept., 1904

78 *Brig O' Balgownie*

A winter view of this ancient arch shows the bleak setting when this was the only route north from Aberdeen. It was built at a leisurely pace about 1320 and has been repaired and modified several times since. It has reverted to its original use as a footbridge.

The Brig O'Balgownie.

A guid New Year an' mony o' them.

79 *Stoneywood Paper Mill*

James Moir set up a paper mill in the Stoneywood estate, which he already owned, in 1770. A year later it was controlled by Alexander Smith and his son-in-law Patrick Pirie. Alexander Pirie, a grandson, developed the mill over a fifty-year period, introducing watermarks; continuous production and white paper made from rags. This aerial view has been taken well before 1992 when the company merged with Wiggins Teape and Co. Other mills on the Don include Donside and Mogiemoss.

AEROFILMS SERIES   STONEYWOOD PAPER MILLS OF ALEX. PIRIE & SONS LTD., BUCKSBURN, ABERDEENSHIRE

80 *Salt fish*

This card shows the process of curing white fish. The fish were gutted, lightly salted then wind-dried. The dried fish were bundled like straw and used as cattle feed or fish meal.

37675   ABERDEEN : " DRYING SALT FISH "   VALENTINES SERIES

81 **Bridge of Dee**

Looking south from the Bridge of Dee, this card was posted in 1917. There are just a few houses at the foot of the bridge and the Railway Bridge is visible in the distance. This well-known bridge dates from 1520, but is has been repaired and widened over the years. It is largely granite with sandstone used for detailed work.

Bridge of Dee, Looking South, Aberdeen

82 *King George Bridge*

King George VI Bridge was opened on 10 March 1941 by the King himself. It shows rusticated granite blocks to a Sir Frank Mears design.

55.   KING GEORGE VI. BRIDGE, ABERDEEN.

83 Convent of the Sacred Heart

In 1895 Rev. Mother Stuart and Rev. Mother Digby visited Aberdeen with a view to founding a convent for their order, the Society of the Sacred Heart. These nuns later gave their name to the highly regarded Digby-Stuart teachers training college in Roehampton in Surrey. They purchased a house called Westwood in Queens Cross, seen in this early postcard. On 13 January 1896 a Convent day school opened with six pupils.

Convent of the Sacred Heart", Aberdeen.
Saint Joseph's House. (South Side).

The Convent school has continued to expand, purchasing neighbouring properties and offering a variety of courses. For many years there was a boarding school but it was closed in 1971. The Golden Jubilee Yearbook of 1945 quotes a former pupil on 'the lack of solitude is a necessary privation in a boarding school and helps to train us to subordinate our tastes and interest to the general good, and to live in harmony with others'. Such sentiments seem very old fashioned today.

"Convent of the Sacred Heart" Aberdeen. The Reading Room.

85 *Kings College air view*

In 1495 Bishop Elphinstone asked Pope Alexander VI to establish a university in Old Aberdeen. The Bull, the formal document approving this, is still in the university achieves. This quickly became known as Kings College. In 1860 the college merged with the younger Marischell College to form the University of Aberdeen.

KING'S COLLEGE
(FROM THE AIR) ABERDEEN

A set of bells dated 1519 were installed in the tower, which was probably completed shortly afterwards. It was rebuilt in 1636. In the chapel the choir stalls decorations include the marguerite in honour of the king's wife, Margaret Tudor. Margaret, sister of King Henry VII of England, forms the link that enables the current Royal family to be able to claim decent from King Alfred. The unusual crown to the tower was constructed at the same time as the similar structure on St. Giles Cathedral in Edinburgh.

King's College, Aberdeen in 1812

87 Kings College window

The window, described as showing 'flamboyant mouchettes and massive central mullions' may have been influenced by foreign designs. Work on the chapel began in 1500 and reflects the cosmopolitan nature of Christianity at that period blending overseas influences with local craftsmanship.

Window in King's College, Aberdeen.   20546.J.V.

88 Student

In 1904 students were still required to deposit £1 if they wished to borrow books from the University library. This young man appears prosperous, but in the period from the 1860's to the 1880's undernourishment was considered commonplace among students.

Student
Aberdeen University.

Aberdeen
Aug 29 03.
I met
Mother & M.S.
here this
morning, we
have been
all round
the town,
am leaving
for Arbroath
by the 5.30
wish you
were here.
Love
from
Flo.

89 *High Street, Old Aberdeen*

In the background is the granite Town House of Old Aberdeen, which was made redundant by the amalgamation of 1891. Old Aberdeen had received a charter from King James IV in 1489 granting the status of a Burgh of Barony, which among other matters established a weekly market and a bi-annual fair. The building constructed in the 1700's has had a variety of uses over the years including being a prison and a water cistern. Several houses in the High Street are older than the Town House. The Post Office can be seen on the left of the road originally called the Via Regia.

POST OFFICE AND HIGH STREET, OLD ABERDEEN

90   St. Machar's Cathedral

An unusual view of the back of St. Machar's, showing part of the graveyard. The card was posted in 1911. There have been Bishops in Aberdeen since about 1130. The building is a mixture of red Sandstone of 1370 and Granite of 1440 and modern changes. The lead was taken from the roof in 1567 but the central tower did not fall until 1688. A new East End arrested the destruction of the building and the fine pre-Reformation roof of the nave remains to this day.

East Window, Old Machar Cathedral, Aberdeen.

91 *Provost Skene's house*

Built from rough granite blocks and dressed free-stone, this townhouse dates back to 1545. It had several owners before George Skene in 1669. He was Provost between 1676 and 1685, receiving a knighthood in 1681. He undertook a major recon-struction of the property, adding turrets and the strange flat roof. Unfortu-nately modern buildings now close this view.

PROVOST SKENE'S HOUSE, ABERDEEN, FROM SOUTH.

The house boasts a ceiling dating from the early 1600's which shows scenes from the Bible, in this case the Crucifixion. Some cards title this 'Cumberland's house' though the Butcher of Colluden only requisitioned it for a few weeks as he moved north. Its use as the Corporation Lodging House does not appear to have been recorded on cards.

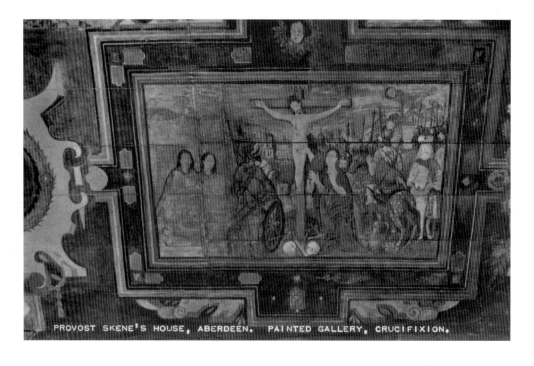

PROVOST SKENE'S HOUSE, ABERDEEN.   PAINTED GALLERY, CRUCIFIXION.

93 Crown Street

A retired Aberdonian engineer tells me that this cards reminds him of the night he blew up the electricity station. During the Second World War he served in a famous Scottish regiment. In 1941 an exercise was arranged where by a different regiment would guard Aberdeen from Commando attacks. The raiding party landed at Cove from a small boat, clambered inland to the railway line and followed it into Aberdeen. They found that, although all the road bridges were guarded, there was no sentry on the Railway Bridge. They marched right to the rear of the electricity works, climbed in and left a dummy bomb before making their escape to the main beach where their boat took them off.

CROWN STREET AND ELECTRICITY WORKS, ABERDEEN

94 *Unitarian Church*

In 1833 Aberdeen-born Rev. Archibald McDonald preached to thousands and left a Unitarian Society of 24 members in the city. Initially meetings were in private houses and then a church in George Street. The congregation grew mainly among the poor. In time they built this 600-seat church. October 1905 saw the memorial stone laid by MP Sir J.T. Brunner Bart on a cold and breezy day. The stone had been positioned by a steam crane and under it were a variety of items including hymn books and daily papers such as the Aberdeen Daily Journal, a list of

benefactors and accepted tenders. The MP used the traditional mallet and silver trowel for the ceremony, which was presented to him by a daughter of the late Mr. Robert 'Rad-ical' Robertson, a founder of the first Unitarian Church in Aberdeen. Today it is occupied by the Jehovah's Witnesses.

Laying Memorial Stone, Unitarian Church, Aberdeen, 30/9/05

95 Clifton Road

The card shows an empty view of Clifton Road. We have seen a card of Anderson Free Library further down the road. The library was donated by Sir John Anderson in 1883 and is the Woodside Library of today.

Clifton Road from Hilton St. — Aberdeen

96 *Great Western Road*

A quiet day on this main road, is seen in this un-posted card.

GREAT WESTERN ROAD (LOOKING WEST), ABERDEEN

97 *Mid Stocket Road*

Parson James Gordon's map of 1661 shows this as the 'way to the Stoked Heade'. It was originally part of the Stocket Forest, one of the hunting grounds given to the city in 1313 by a grateful Robert the Bruce.

2067 - MID STOCKET ROAD, ABERDEEN, LOOKING EAST

Woodhouse Bar, McKilligan's Corner, Stoneywood is seen at the turn of the century when it was still safe to play in the streets. McKilligan had been a barman at the Station Hotel (now the Staging Post), but saved enough to buy this bar. There used to be a living room on the ground floor and later a small shop. The cottages behind the bar have gone, but it is still in business.

99 Queens Cross

The Aberdeen Land Association, established in 1875, purchased land in this area, laying out an extension to the city. Fountainhall Road to the right was originally North Swithern Street.

No. 15.   QUEEN'S CROSS, ABERDEEN.   THE ADELPHI SERIES.
C. H. & S. A.

Elm Hill House Asylum
can be glimpsed in the distance. Originally there was
a 'bedlam' for the mad at
Clarkseat, in the Berryden
and Elmhill area. The bedlam opened in 1800 with
twelve eight feet square
cells, but this institution
was for wealthier patients.

CEDAR PLACE, ABERDEEN

101 *The Well, Victoria Park*

There used to be many wells in the city, this one in Victoria Park. This is the city's oldest park, dating from 1871, and it was formed from four fields covering 14 acres.

The Well, Victoria Park, Aberdeen

102 Stewart Park

This park opened in 1894 and is named after the then Lord Provost of Aberdeen, Sir David Stewart. Mrs. Taylor of Woodside had left £500 for a play area and this was used to buy 14 acres close to Hilton House. Within the land acquired from the Hilton estate were three disused quarries, which were retained in part to make ponds that were stocked with fish. These have since been filled in but the park still provides opportunities for games and a quiet stroll enjoying the flowers.

Stewart Park Woodside.   near Aberdeen

103 Duthie Park

Duthie Park was presented to the city by Miss Duthie in 1873. An earlier owner of the land had been Arthur Dingwall Fordyce, who gave his name to the house, Arthur's Seat. The statue of Hygeia was made in Jute Street by mason James Philip.

236. STATUE OF HYGEIA IN DUTHIE PARK, ABERDEEN   THE ADELPHI SERIES.
G. H. & S. A.

104 *Heather Day*

'Gala and Heather Day Sunday August 22 1915' was the name given to a pair of events to raise money for the Aberdeen Royal Infirmary. A great Gala was held in Duthie Park for which admission cost six pence. Attendance was estimated at 25,000 or 26,000, a significant proportion of the city. At the time it was the largest event that had ever been arranged in the park. Individual activities included a musical drill by a team of ladies, displays of physical drill by a squad from the Gordon Highlanders, exhibition dances and a motor cycle gymkhana. In addition, 1,500 people sold sprigs of heather on the streets of Aberdeen raising £474, bringing the total for the day to over £1,000.

Gala and Heather Day in the Duthie Park.
21st August, 1915.

Adelphi Series

105 *Westburn Park*

Aberdeen is a city keen on sport, in this case tennis. The park was purchased by the city in 1899 and became a public park two years later. It has been used as the venue for the Lawn Bowl World Championships.

WESTBURN PARK, THE TENNIS COURTS, ABERDEEN 3036

106 *Hazlehead Park*

The Hazlehead estate was purchased from the Rose family in 1920 for £20,000. It has been much changed over the years, with a golf course added in 1927 costing as much as the original purchase. This card shows putting and was posted in 1932.

THE PUTTING COURSE, HAZLEHEAD, ABERDEEN

74

107 Golf on the Links

The earliest reference to golf in Aberdeen is in 1625 and a Society of Golfers was founded in 1780. In 1647 there was a plague in Aberdeen resulting in over 1,700 deaths. A number of the graves of victims were found on the Links about two hundred years later, during sewer laying. In 1875 a Mr. Bloxsom completed 12 rounds on the links in a single day. In a more leisurely fashion, on a card posted in 1935, golfers are enjoying a fine day by the sea.

BRIDGE OF DON, ABERDEEN.

206449.J.V.

108 *Sandilands Chemical Works*

John Miller & Co, Sandilands, was taken over by ICI in 1928. Located next to the gas works, the chemical works utilized waste products of its neighbour. The gasholders contained 500,000 cubic feet each in 1953, at which time the chemical output included 1,550 tons of sulphate of ammonia, 10,000 of tar and three million gallons of Benzole. Miller Street is at this end of the view. Directors of the works including members of the Miller family are listed on this unused card.

AERIAL PHOTOS LTD.   SANDILANDS CHEMICAL WORKS   EDINBURGH
                                      FROM AN AEROPLANE.

109 *Grandholm Mill*

In 1859 Crombies took over the Grandholm woollen mill of Leys, Masson & Co and it remained in Crombie family control until 1893. The company prospered under the direction of Alexander Ross and his son John, who established an excellent reputation for community service. The firm's customer list included not just the British Army but the Russian and Confederate Armies as well. A progressive company, Crombie employed 1,200 in the 1920s and provided paid holidays and sick pay in the 1930s. In 1983 a Visitor Centre opened, but in recent years the site has scaled down.

GRANDHOLM MILLS, WOODSIDE, ABERDEEN

110 *Barracks*

The Bridge of Don Barracks was the home of the local regiment from 1935 to 1960. The barracks were struck by an air raid on 21 April 1942. 27 servicemen died and a further 26 were injured. In time it became the Training Depot of the Scottish Division.

BRIDGE OF DON BARRACKS, ABERDEEN

71

111 Mannie o' the Well

This well was also known as the 'Mannie o' the Green' where it stood from 1852 to 1958. It had been in the Castlegate from 1708 – some sources say 1706 – to where it returned in 1972. It takes its name from the lead statue on top.

The United Free South Church, nowadays St. Mark's Church, was built in 1892. A. Marshall MacKenzie created this sombre interior which is alleged inspired by a German church. Part of the great 'Education, Salvation, Damnation' trio, the interior is uncommon on cards.

INTERIOR, ST. MARK'S, ABERDEEN.

113 **The Howes**

The Howes at Bucksburn shows a rural view.

The Howes, Bucksburn.

In 1862 six nuns of the Congregation of the Poor Sisters of Nazareth arrived in Aberdeen from London and undertook to care for the aged and infirm of both sexes irrespective of creed. They also cared for orphans and incurable children. They depended upon the generosity of local residents for funds. The convent church shown in this 1938 card was built by Charles McGrigor at his own expense and opened on 23 January 1873 and includes a replica of the statue in Reims known as Our Lady of Aberdeen.

CHAPEL, NAZARETH HOUSE, ABERDEEN.

115 *Baths*

The Bon Accord Baths measure 120 x 42 feet and are 15 feet deep. There are diving platforms to 33 feet. It was designed by the city architect and opened in 1940, being frequently described as a granite box. 1,000 spectators can be seated at the Justice Mill Lane site, often called the Uptown Baths.

BON-ACCORD BATHS, ABERDEEN

116 **Milkman**

Whitefield Dairy were based at 9 Baker Street from 1902 to the 1920's. The dairymen were listed as Mr. Tough and Mr. Winchester, but we have not identified this individual. From the dates on other cards this photograph was probably taken in 1904. One of the advantages of horses for milk-carts is that the horse would walk to the next delivery point whilst the milkman was down a path. You never had to walk back to collect your float!

117   *Fruits sellers*

The Green kept its role as a market place well into the era of postcards. Beyond the original bounds of the community, it lies on the way from the riverside to the higher ground with the kirk and castle. Now a backwater, the Green is overshadowed by recent developments.

Fruitsellers, The Green, Aberdeen

118 *Mercat Cross*

Scotland's finest cross was built in 1686 some distance west of its present position before being moved in 1842. At earlier periods the cross has been used as a post office and by stallholders. In the panels above the arches can be seen portraits of the Stewart monarchs and beyond the cross George Duncan's shop. This is a Tuck card from their Silverette series.

119 *Gallery*

When the gallery was extended in 1905 over two hundred plaster casts of famous statues were constructed. The granite pillars, many locally donated, are real.

Sculpture Gallery, Aberdeen.   The Central Hall.

120 *Fire station*

The Fire station in Kings Road was constructed during the tenure of Lord Provost Daniel Mearns, and cost £16,500. The building dates from 1899. We see some of the 23 fire fighters of the period with horse-drawn tenders, which did not completely disappear until the 1920's. Aberdeen recently made national headlines with their decision to paint Fire Service vehicles white. This colour is cheaper than the traditional red paint. Grampian Fire Brigade now employs over 800 staff tackling over 8,000 emergencies a year.

FIRE BRIGADE STATION, ABERDEEN.

121 *Middle School*

The Middle School was one of the group of schools built during the decade following the establishment of the Schools Board in 1872. It was the scene of the Great Haircut Riot. It used to be the practice of school medical officers to give haircuts to verminous children. On 16 June 1919 a crowd of about 200 angry mothers gathered outside the Middle School where girls were being deloused without their parents being warned. Minor breakages occurred. Further disturbances took place throughout the day but within two days all the pupils were back in class. The tower belongs to the university. Middle School, originally Gallowgate School, closed in 1975 after exactly one hundred years.

MIDDLE SCHOOL AND MARISCHAL COLLEGE, ABERDEEN

122 *Union Grove*

This street is named after Union Grove, the home of Provost Hadden and his family. In earlier times there was a dam here which provided water to the Upper Justice Mill for centuries. St. Nicholas, Union Grove (Church of Scotland), was still the St. Nicholas United Presbyterian Church in 1894 when it celebrated its centenary. At that time the kirk's best-known personality was Miss Janet Melville, who organized a famously effective Sunday School for many years. A woman of outstanding character and personality whom gave a lifelong example of prac-tical Christianity. Her life story can be found in D.P. Thomson's 'Women of the Scottish Church'.

The building is now flats.

UNION GROVE, ABERDEEN   VALENTINES SERIES

123 *Woodside School*

Woodside School re-presented the latest in school architecture when it was built in 1902. It was only two stories high and offered plenty of light and ventilation and was even well heated. It cost £18,000 but as it took 1,537 pupils it was good value. The author's wife re-members the 1950's at this school with affection.

124 *War Memorial*

On 29 September 1923
the Moderators of the
Church of Scotland and
the United Free Church
dedicated the War Memor-
ial. King George V opened
Cowdray Hall and other
extensions on the same
day. Lord and Lady Cow-
dray had paid for the hall
and thus earned the hon-
our of the Freedom of
the City. This was con-
ferred on 3 May 1927;
with a luncheon at the
Town and County Hall
where the menu included
salmon, roast chicken and
foie gras on toast, to the
strains of light classical
music.

3023.

War Memorial, Aberdeen.

125 *Victoria Bridge*

There was a ferry accident on 5 April 1876, which finally prompted the erection of the Victoria Bridge. 32 or 33 (accounts vary) died when a small ferry carrying sixty passengers overturned. The new bridge opened on 2 July 1881 at the cost of £25,000. A considerable expansion of Torry followed, some of which can be seen in the next two cards.

Victoria Bridge, Aberdeen

126 *Menzies Street*

The Menzies family owned much of Nigg from about 1750. In 1875 the city acquired all the land to the east of Mansefield Road. The Menzies kept the rest and gave their name to this street. The card shows the corner of Walker Street with A. W. Scott, fruitier, and was published by J. Anderson, 7 Menzies Street in 1925.

MENZIES RD, TORRY LOOKING DOWN.

127 *Victoria Street*

Archibald Simpson laid out Victoria Street in Torry as the community grew in the nineteenth century with the booming trawling industry. Torry had a Charter as a Burgh of Barony from about 1495, which entitled the burgh to hold a weekly market and control trades and crafts in the area. Torry merged with the city in 1891, but did not see a motor bus service until 1921.

VICTORIA ROAD, ABERDEEN.

128 Blenheim Place

A quiet street typical of
this part of the city.

BLENHEIM PLACE, ABERDEEN

129 *Holborn Street School*

Holborn Street School was a Primary or Intermediate (sources differ) School seen in this G. W. Wilson card from about 1905. It was demolished and the Aberdeen Commercial College built on the site. That has now also gone to be replaced by office buildings.

Holburn Street School, Aberdeen

Annie, Viscountess Cowdray, gave the Club to the Royal College of Nursing as a residential and social club for nurses and other professional women in 1929. In Fonthill Road, the Club and the adjacent Fonthill Lodge have been tastefully renovated with the dining room and ballroom being particularly gracious. The Club provides nursing care ranging from a few days rest to full dependency nursing. Residents may rest assured that it no longer has this dated appearance but provides first class accommodation in the two buildings.

DRAWING ROOM - COWDRAY CLUB

131 Horses

A horseman is seen with his horses at Little Arnage. One horse required the same amount of food as six humans but produced ten times as much work. Until the introduction of tractors after World War Two, horses were the essential element in Aberdeenshire agriculture.

132 *Besam Jamie*

A local street trader is selling besams on this card. An other card in the same series shows a 'rabbity' seller.

Besom Jamie, The Heather King.

133 *Lord Roberts*

Field Marshall Lord Roberts of Kandahar, on the right of this picture, is seen reviewing a march past at the Music Hall. He was made a Burgess of the City in 1913 and this is one of a series of cards to commemorate his visit. He had replaced the Commander-in chief in South Africa and defeated the Boers. He was over 80 by this time, having won a Victoria Cross during the Indian Mutiny. He died from pneumonia in 1914 whilst visiting the Western Front.

134 Lord Robert's crowd
This card shows the
throng who waited to see
the military hero.

135 *Castle Hill Barracks*

AG.W. Wilson card and the only postcard view we have ever seen of the exterior of the castle and barracks. A castle stood here from the 1100's. The barracks were erected in 1794 and used by the Gordon Highlanders until 1935. After many years of neglect they were demolished in 1965 to provide space for a pair of tower blocks.

Castlehill Barracks, Aberdeen

The hostels, seen on a card posted in 1940, provide accommodation to students at the Northern College. Many a future teacher has had their first taste of life away from home in these buildings.

CLIFTON AND HILTON HOSTELS, WOODSIDE, ABERDEEN

62

137 *Rowett Institute*

The Institute was constituted in 1913 and work began in 1914 to be quickly suspended until 1919. An American, reputed to be a rum smuggler, Dr. John Quiller Rowett gifted the land. The first buildings opened in 1922, including laboratories and a library. The Institute included the Duthie experimental stock farm of 600 acres and 400 acres of hill pasture. It provides useful links between veterinary and human sciences plus public health and agriculture. Perhaps John Boyd Orr undertook its most famous work in the 1930's demonstrating the link between income and diet. He also showed that compared with the English, Scottish people eat three times as much syrup, treacle, jam and marmalade.

ROWETT INSTITUTE NEAR STONEYWOOD, ABERDEEN.   204506.J.V.

138 *Stoneywood Church*

Stoneywood Church opened in 1879 at the cost of £4,000, which was finally paid following a large bazaar in 1887. This was a three-day affair held at the Music Hall, which raised £810. It provided places for 820 people and the Earl of Aberdeen played a prominent role in fund raising. In the early 1990's, after the building had been vacant for some time, it was converted into office space. The window is still intact but this fine organ was given away.

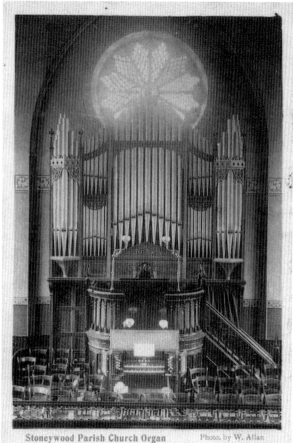

Stoneywood Parish Church Organ   Photo. by W. Allan

This is the organ of the church here a very pretty one it is

139 Lorry

A Sentinel DG4 is shown painted up for deliver to Mutter Howey & Co of Charlotte Street and Guild Street. This type of steam lorry was in production from 1926 to 1935. After 1931 pneumatic tyres were optional but this vehicle has solid tyres and chain drive. With a vertical boiler and Duplex engine, its 11 foot 6 inch wheelbase could carry six or seven tons.

140 **An Aberdeenshire family**

Photographed outside the family farm in Ellon is the Stephen family who later stayed in Aberdeen. James Stephen (born in 1866) and his wife Agnes Rait (born in 1873) are flanked by most of their children. Jessie 'Janey' (born in 1914), the author's mother-in-law, appears about nine years old so the postcard dates to about 1923. Many of the family's descendants still live in Aberdeen.